This book belongs to

_____

Field Guide to the Soul

Field Guide to the Soul

An Inspired Activity Book to
Help You Find Peace, Purpose &
Connection through the Magical
Teachings of Nature

MANDY FORD

BETTER DAY BOOKS®

Field Guide to the Soul © 2023 by
Mandy Ford and Better Day Books, Inc.

Publisher: Peg Couch
Book Designer: Llara Pazdan
Editor: Colleen Dorsey

Library of Congress Control
Number: 2022943930

ISBN: 978-0-7643-6656-7
Printed in China
First printing

Copublished by Better Day Books,
Inc., and Schiffer Publishing, Ltd.

Attributions for quotes in
artwork: pages 16–17: Rumi;
pages 40–41: Mary Oliver;
pages 52–53: Rumi; pages
88–89: Mary Oliver

BETTER DAY BOOKS®

Better Day Books
P.O. Box 21462
York, PA 17402
Phone: 717-487-5523
Email: hello@betterdaybooks.com
www.betterdaybooks.com
 @better_day_books

Schiffer Publishing
4880 Lower Valley Road
Atglen, PA 19310
Phone: 610-593-1777
Fax: 610-593-2002
Email: info@schifferbooks.com
www.schifferbooks.com

This title is available for promotional or commercial use,
including special editions. Contact info@schifferbooks.com
for more information.

Dedication

To Dan, Ben, and Landon:

Thank you for being my home and safe
space, showing me what is possible,
keeping me grounded, and always
cheering me on.

Contents

Welcome

ello, dear soul. Welcome to a dream that's been rooting, growing, and taking shape in your heart for years, even if you didn't realize it.

I am inviting you on a journey to expand your soul, embrace the miraculous, find truth in nature, and allow the Universe to guide you into living a more authentic, joyful life. Your soul's purpose is waiting for you to discover it, embrace it, and nurture it.

Through the lens of the natural world and through heartfelt self-reflection, this book will help guide you along your own soul's path. Find a comfortable seat, take a few deep breaths, and come along with me. You will encounter magical stars, comforting clouds, and encouraging mountain views; you will flow along with water and wind, feel the warm magic of the sun, and be nurtured by the comfort and stability of the forest and the moon.

Nature is always there, showing you how easy it can be to show up simply as you are, and reminding you that although change is constant, there is always a comforting presence available to you as you navigate this life.

You will learn in these pages how everything around you is magical and filled with the positive energy of the Universe. You will discover that you are always being guided and constantly supported.

You are not alone on this journey of being human, my friend.

My wish for you is to feel the encouraging embrace of the Universe, showing you that no matter what, your soul knows the way.

My own personal journey took many years to lead me to writing this book, years in which I was able to reconnect with my passions and grow my authentic soul. The seed was first planted in the spring of 2013, when I audited a creative writing course at the college where I worked. I signed up for the class because a dear friend was the professor, and I wanted to soak up as much time with her as I could before she moved back home to Nashville. What I didn't know at the time was how that class would lead me back to my soul's purpose. When I walked into the classroom on the first day, I felt a strange sense of knowing. It was comforting and hopeful, and it was a sensation I had never experienced before. It felt electric, flowing through my body from head to toe.

I knew I was embarking on something life-changing, but I had no idea what that something would look like. It was such a palpable feeling, and yet I had no evidence other than just, well, knowing! It enveloped me like a warm hug in a time when a lot of life's circumstances felt scary and uncertain. My soul knew a lovely secret that it wasn't quite ready to share with me yet—a tiny seed of a dream being held safely by the Universe. And the secret was this: I would soon be coming back to my art and embarking on the biggest creative journey of my life.

That journey has brought me here, writing these words and creating this art for you. It feels miraculous and yet, at the same time, not surprising at all. There is so much we don't know about how and where we are being guided, but we *are* being guided, and I want you to feel and know this truth too.

My hope is that you will make this book your own. You can journey your way through in the chapter order or allow yourself to be guided to whatever spot feels right to you. You may be in the mood to read, journal, or do a meditation, or perhaps you simply need to open the book to a piece of art and allow the imagery to soak into your soul. Let your intuition guide you to whatever message you need to experience.

Each chapter includes something interactive for you to do—a meditation, a page to fill with journaling, a place to use your imagination to create something new. And each chapter ends with a set of affirmations you can adopt into your daily life. Mark up the pages, add your hopes and dreams, and claim this space as your sacred place to manifest your own soul's magic.

Your tiny seed of a dream is waiting for you.

And now it's time for your journey to begin.

CHAPTER 1

Dream

Do you believe the Universe is on your side and supporting your dreams? It can be hard to trust that we are being divinely guided, but I am here to tell you this magical force of energy is real, and it is ready to envelop you with love and encouragement!

If you are like me, and playing it safe is your comfort zone, you may experience quite a bit of discomfort, anxiety, and maybe even fear when life throws big changes your way, or even when you are simply contemplating making a change. All of a sudden, you are faced with a new reality that can feel surreal and frightening. Or you may be ready for a change but are finding it difficult to commit to taking the first step. You might be feeling stuck and unsure what the next right thing to do should be. What will bring you fulfillment and purpose? What is your soul's calling, and how can you find your way down that path? How do you know you are making the right choices?

Life is a mix of constant flow and change, and the path isn't always clear or straight. There are obstacles to navigate, and you can be faced with tough decisions. Knowing this, you may ask yourself if it is truly possible to do the work you feel called to do in this world—work that is ridiculously fun and fulfilling—and create a life around that.

The Universe knows the answer is YES! All you have to do is be open to receiving what is already available to you.

They say that whatever is meant for us will not pass us by, no matter what we do to delay it or push it away. I'm not sure if that is always true, but I am here to tell you that it happened for me, and I believe it can happen for you too.

I want you to hear the Universe saying, "I know what your soul needs. Let me find a way for you to get closer to that reality."

• • •

All you have to do is be open to receiving what is already available to you.

• • •

You are the ecstatic

Universe in motion.

Reflection

There are somewhere between 200 billion to two trillion galaxies in the Universe, and scientific evidence shows we are made of the same stuff as the stars. How amazing and mind-blowing is that? And if those things are true, then it feels totally possible for so many other magical things to happen. Why not believe that our soul can live the life of its dreams?

It is up to you to discern what that life will look like, and I can guarantee that yours will be as unique as the stars and as unique as your soul. There is not one other soul like yours.

In order to receive these wonderful, dreamy gifts from the Universe, we must first trust that it can happen, and believe that we are already worthy of a life full of meaning and enjoyment.

I trust the Universe to guide me.

What can you trust the Universe to provide for you? What is your soul dreaming of? Take some time, right now, to dream.

Write down anything and everything that comes to your mind when you think of your "dream" life. What lights you up? What would you do with your time if you didn't need to worry about bills, or health insurance, or any of those worldly, adult things that bog us all down?

_____

_____

_____

_____

_____

_____

_____

_____

_____

Activity: Stargazing Meditation

On a clear night, go outside (a window view will also work), get comfortably seated, and look up at the stars. Find one star to connect with and focus on that one bright light. Choose a star that feels right—you'll know it when you see it!

Take a few deep breaths and imagine that you are transported up into the sky, getting up close and personal and connecting with your star.

What color is it? What does it feel like? Is it warm and welcoming?

Imagine the light of your star enveloping you with positive energy. Maybe even give the star a name so you can feel a deeper connection (or look up its name on a star map).

Now take a few moments to talk to your star.

Tell it your dreams. Share your wishes for your soul, as well as your fears. Allow all your words to be received by your star and consumed by its magical light. You are now connected to and supported by your star!

Allow yourself to feel the magic of the connection and support you are being given by the Universe.

Sit with this feeling for as long as you need. Repeat this meditation whenever you start to doubt your magic.

Affirmations

You've spent time writing down your dreams, and you've shared them with the Universe. There is a tremendous amount of positive energy generated when we put words and a voice to our dreams!

You have now claimed your power as a unique creature, one with a soul created to do magical things here on Earth. You are as unique as the stars, you were put here for a purpose, and you are magic!

Repeat these affirmations when doubt starts to creep in:

I am a unique and magical creature

I was created for a purpose

I can manifest a life of meaning

I am worthy of my dreams

I am magic

Let's keep going and figure out how to make that magic happen in the most authentically "you" way!

What is
the
dream
of your
soul?

CHAPTER 2

Grow

Have you ever noticed the amount of time it takes for a dream or goal to come to fruition? There are often many steps involved over a prolonged period of time. As much as becoming an overnight sensation appeals to us, such successes are usually paired with a long history of work behind the scenes. This process may be a test of our patience, but it is also where the magic happens!

Your ideas and dreams have a gestation period. They need time to hang out underground, in the warm embrace of your soul, until they are ready to sprout and make their way out into the world. This growth period can be challenging to accept at times and super frustrating when you are in the middle of it and want to see things happen.

You might know what the end goal is, but you either aren't sure exactly how to get there or you need to complete so many steps to make it to the finish line that it feels like you'll never arrive. I, too, have struggled with finding patience in this process.

The good news is that the Universe has an infinite amount of patience. Isn't that a relief? We can stomp our feet, sigh deeply, and roll our eyes as much as we want, but as long as we balance those naturally human reactions with a heavy dose of trust in the process, that seed we planted will continue to sprout and grow at the right pace to be healthy and in perfect timing.

You may also find yourself feeling fiercely protective of your sprouting dream. That is a good thing! While you may want to shout from the rooftops about this amazing thing you are working on, allow me to encourage you to think about another way to cheer on your sacred, magical dream: keep it close and quiet.

I'd like to challenge you to allow only the best of energies to surround your seed and help it grow. Then it becomes a super-secret project that is between only you, the Universe, and people who you know will hold it with the same care and positive energy as you do. Later, once your dream has sprouted and taken shape, it can be shared with the world!

. . .

The Universe has
an infinite amount
of patience.

. . .

Protect your *growing dream*

Reflection

Take some time to think of a dream or goal you are holding close in your heart—something you want to happen or are currently working toward that feels super sacred.

Now, think about whom you feel safe sharing that dream with. Remember, keep it close and quiet! Maybe for now it needs to stay between you, your soul, and the Universe. Or perhaps there are one or two people you can trust with it.

Write down your dream here and journal for a bit about how you can protect it while it grows.

_____

_____

_____

_____

_____

_____

_____

_____

_____

_____

_____

_____

Activity:
Dream Vision Map

Use these pages to envision your goal and what you need to keep it growing. Write your dream in the center (the seed). In the innermost circle around the seed, write the names of people you feel safe sharing your dream with, as well as what you need to nurture your dream. As you move further away from the seed, write down people and things that correspond to those layers.

close + quiet

my dream

Affirmations

I hope this chapter has helped you identify the dream you are growing, envision it as a seed needing careful tending and nourishing, and create and cultivate boundaries that will help your dream grow and thrive. It is very important to protect your dream and to remember how amazing it is that you have been trusted with its creation!

If you need a simple practice to stick with this process, find a few quiet moments and repeat these affirmations:

**My dream is worthy of
my care and support**

**My dream is worthy of
the care and support of others**

My dream is sacred

I will keep my dream close and quiet

**I will protect my dream and
surround it with positive
energy while it grows**

When the Universe conspires with you to grow and bring forth a sacred dream, you owe it your precious time and energy to make sure it thrives in the world. This is part of your soul's journey!

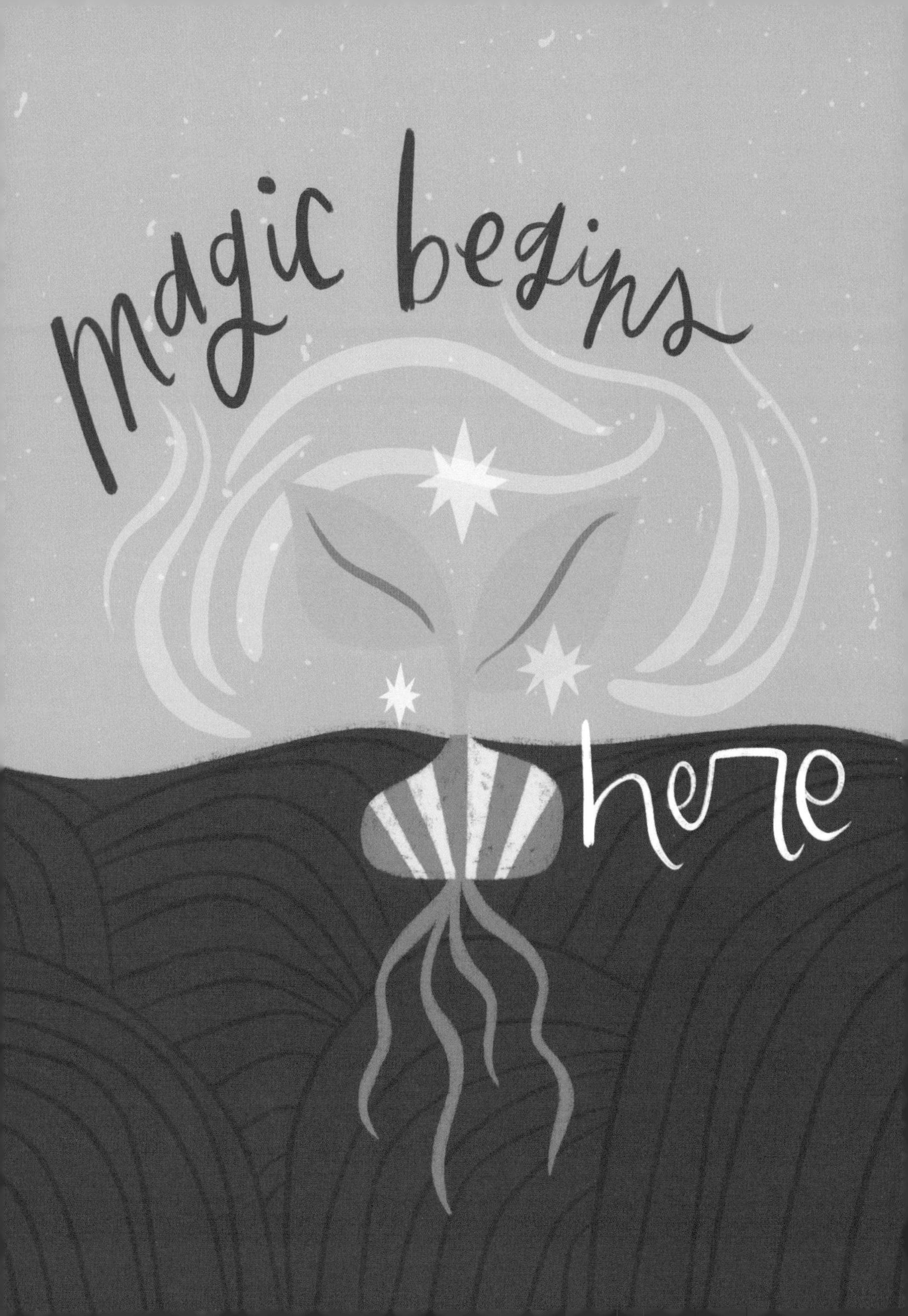
magic begins
here

CHAPTER 3

Explore

*T*he beginning of a new adventure can be scary, especially if you can't see the path ahead of you. That's how most adventures happen! You are moving happily along, and then you are struck with an unexpected plot twist that requires you to adapt. Or maybe it was your choice to take a leap. Chosen change can still be super scary and anxiety-inducing, and it can bring about so many questions.

What if it doesn't work out? What if you lose your way? What if you don't have the support you need?

The good news is that you always have the support you need. It may not be in physical form, but every second of every day you are supported by unseen, divine forces that are joining you on our path. They are with you in the valley when you are tired and achy and unsure how to keep going. And they are with you on the mountaintop when your dream has come to fruition and you are radiating with positive energy and joy.

Even more importantly, they are with you in the ordinary, quiet moments—the parts of life that feel boring and unremarkable.

These are actually some of the most important moments! You are doing the incremental work to move yourself along the path from valley to mountaintop and back again. These moments make up the bulk of your life, but they are so often overlooked because they aren't shiny or exciting. Truly, though, they hold the most value for your soul's growth.

You are growing in the quiet times, in the loud times, and in each moment in the spaces in between. Allow yourself to be present and mindful of each step of your journey. Enjoy the scenery, smell the air, listen for the sounds of the Universe calling you, and "be astonished" with your life (as Mary Oliver said). It is all a miracle, and it all matters.

• • •

You are growing in the quiet times,
in the loud times, and in each
moment in the spaces in between.

• • •

Reflection

Take some time now to think about the quiet, everyday moments you experience—the daily tasks and mundane activities that are woven together into the fabric of your life. List some of those things here.

_____

_____

_____

_____

_____

Think about the valleys and the mountaintops.

What have you achieved and celebrated? What have you mourned, lost, or discarded? List a few of those things here.

_____

_____

_____

_____

_____

Now think about how all these moments are connected. Do you see the threads that have woven them all together as you move forward on your soul's journey? You cannot have one without the other. Take a few moments to reflect on the significance of it all.

_____

_____

_____

_____

_____

_____

_____

_____

_____

_____

_____

Activity: Following the Path

In a quiet moment, use your finger to slowly make your way along the path. Take your time. Picture what you will find at the end. What is your soul seeking? It can be something tangible or simply a feeling. Imagine your body moving along the path, allowing your senses to be completely encompassed by the experience. Once you've reached the end, sit and meditate on how you feel.
How can this path be a metaphor for your life?

Start

Affirmations

Approaching life from an explorer's frame of mind allows you to get curious and see the importance in every step of your journey. Your soul is on a grand adventure, and you are holding the compass!

You can discover excitement in the mundane moments and cultivate equilibrium when you find yourself in a high or low period. There is a balance to be found when you realize each moment carries the same amount of importance. That really great thing you achieved? You wouldn't have it without the list of daily tasks you completed to make it happen. And you wouldn't be the same person without having navigated that deep loss or challenging experience.

Here are some affirmations to repeat to yourself when the journey gets rough or you are feeling a bit lost:

I am on a grand adventure

My soul knows the way

I always have the support I need

I will practice being present
in each moment

Every step of my journey
is important

Be present in each moment. Be astonished at what you can achieve and how you can persevere; allow yourself to rest when you need to recharge. Each and every moment is woven together to create a beautiful journey.

CHAPTER 4

Spark

*D*o you have a friendship that feels like coming home? A person whose presence exudes a comfortable, familiar vibe? You aren't quite sure why, but you want to be around this person and soak in their aura. Maybe you even feel like you might have known them in another life. This person gets you and all your quirks, celebrates you and cheers you on, and is there for you with a tissue and a shoulder when things get rough.

A friendship like this, to quote Rumi, "fans your flames."

These friendships are a gift from the Universe. A person who ignites your passions and gives you an extra nudge when you need it is a priceless treasure.

When you are first shown this kind of friendship, you might not be sure how to receive the attention. Feelings of unworthiness could crop up. But the Universe will keep showing up with encouragement and unconditional love to keep you going, continuously fanning the flames of your soul's greatest desires.

Sometimes a friend like this will come along to rekindle a flame that has flickered out within you. You may have forgotten about your light—about a gift your soul was entrusted with upon your birth into this life. The Universe will send this person to ignite the spark of genius that lies deep within you. A spark that you knew was there all along but had forgotten to use amid the craziness of human existence.

Other times, this type of friendship will arrive to introduce you to your spark. The person notices something within you that you have never seen, and suddenly a whole new world of possibility opens. This encouragement is sent to you at exactly the right time, when you are ready and willing to move further into your calling.

Your soul is getting the attention it needs to keep you moving toward the things that feel right. You understand you are worthy, and you are ready to keep growing your flame.

I've seen it happen for me, and I know it can happen for you. Remaining open to these small and sometimes large nudges from the Universe is all you need.

• • •

Your soul is getting the attention it needs to keep you moving toward the things that feel right.

• • •

Reflection

Years ago, during the beginning stages of one of my most beautiful friendships, I was eating lunch with my friend and talking about something heavy. I started to feel tears welling up in my eyes, and I immediately felt awkward and vulnerable. My friend replied with "It's okay, I have tissues!" I knew in that moment this was a friendship I could trust and someone who would encourage me to use every part of my journey to help move me forward into my best life.

Has someone shown up for you like this?

Or has there been an experience where you needed this type of encouragement, and it wasn't available?

you are surrounded by encouragement

How can you show up for others like this too? Think about how you can fan the flames of others and brainstorm some ideas here.

_____

_____

_____

_____

_____

_____

_____

_____

_____

_____

_____

_____

Activity:
Campfire Dreams Visualization

Picture yourself sitting in front of an unlit campfire. There is a neatly arranged pile of firewood in front of you, encircled by smooth, gray stones. You are seated on a cozy blanket facing the logs. Now think of a dream you are working toward, or perhaps one that is still a tiny spark in your mind. Now imagine that spark jumping from your mind and traveling through the air and onto that pile of firewood. This spark alone might be enough to start the fire—but imagine if there were more!

Now think about a person in your life who fits the description of the flame fanner we talked about in this chapter. Envision them sitting across from you, with the campfire between your bodies. As you are sending your sparks into the fire, picture this person fanning the beginnings of the first little flame, blowing gently on it to encourage it to grow.

Picture this person holding a piece of paper with words of encouragement they have written on it. What would be on that piece of paper?

Now picture them taking the paper and dipping its corner into the flame. The note catches fire, and they add it to your growing blaze. If you have more than one person in your life like this, imagine each one of them adding their encouragement to your fire in the same way.

If you are in a spot in life where you don't have a person to fill this role, that is okay! You can create this person—an embodiment of the Universe—to fill this role for you. Even if you don't have a person here in human form to fan your flames, you do have the Universe helping you every second of every day.

You are not alone around this campfire of dream-growing!

Affirmations

Tending the fire of your dreams is challenging work and can feel lonely at times. Knowing the Universe is always on your side and finding friendships that offer unconditional support both make a tremendous difference in nudging you forward and keeping you motivated.

Repeat the following affirmations when your spark needs extra kindling:

I am surrounded
by encouragement

I am worthy of attention and care

A world of possibility
is available to me

The Universe is sending me exactly
what I need in each moment

I am growing the flame of my
dream one spark at a time

Remember that you are surrounded by positive energy on this journey. Take your spark and allow it to grow into a beautiful flame!

CHAPTER 5

Connect

Community and connection are essential for successfully pursuing your dreams over the long term in a healthy and sustainable way, and for giving back to others so that they can pursue their own dreams. Trees, which have always fascinated me, provide the perfect metaphor for this truth.

I recently discovered research by Suzanne Simard on what she calls the "mother tree" and how forests contain magical underground connections beyond our wildest imagination. Their root systems and mycorrhizal networks of fungal roots provide an interconnected community of support for families of trees. And the "mother" of the forest provides a sacred and crucial foundation for all the seedlings surrounding her. She sends them carbon dioxide and water, and she signals when there might be danger. This process mirrors human connection in so many ways.

As you journey through life, there are times when you need a mother tree, and others when *you* are the mother tree. You need to both be sent guidance and also to offer it to those in your community. As you move along on your soul's journey, these connections and root systems are crucial to finding your way and having the resources you need to stay healthy, to branch out and try new things, to shed your leaves when it is time to rest, and to sprout new growth when the time is right.

Human beings are, as Brené Brown says, "hardwired for connection." And, it turns out, so are trees! In so many ways, your needs and capacity to care and grow are a mirror of nature. Your roots may not be physically visible, but they are invisibly woven throughout your relationships, and they both moor you to your place in the world and connect you in a kinship of humankind that is amazingly powerful. The work you do in the world sends out a network of support just as the mother tree does for her forest. It reaches further than you can imagine.

• • •

In so many ways, your needs and capacity to care and grow are a mirror of nature.

• • •

Reflection

Think about a time when you have been in a growing season, in a grieving season, or unsure of what was coming next. Did someone show up for you as a mother tree? What support did you experience to help you on your path? How were your roots strengthened and nourished during this time?

_____

_____

_____

_____

_____

_____

Think about the ways you can and have shown up for others as their mother tree. Perhaps you haven't thought lately about how you can do this for others. Take some time now to think about and write down the ways in which you can offer support to your network of friends and family. How can you be their root system to help them grow and thrive?

Activity:
Envisioning Your Mother Tree

Find a large tree you can sit underneath or a strong image of a tree you can picture in your mind. The tree needs to have a tall, sturdy trunk and limbs that fan out over top of you. This is your mother tree, and her presence feels comforting. You have a bond with this tree.

Sit whatever way is most comfortable underneath your mother tree (or envision yourself doing so), resting your hands on your thighs.

Now think of a situation in your life that is currently unresolved for which you need support.

It may be something you are excited about and want to see come to fruition, or a situation that brings up difficult emotions for which you want to find a resolution.

Focus on your feelings surrounding this situation.

Take a few deep breaths. Visualize the roots of your mother tree coming up from under the ground to meet you where you sit. Feel them providing a sturdy and yet soft place to land. Think about what you need right now, and imagine the roots of your mother tree sending you those exact things to nourish and sustain you on your journey.

Now look up and visualize yourself being covered and supported from above by the branches of your mother tree.

You are bolstered and covered by support from below and above. Sit for a few moments with this feeling. Take a few more deep breaths. Know that you are going to be okay.

Affirmations

It may be tempting to tackle life's problems and challenges on your own, but please don't forget you have a root system to support you. Your own mother tree can show up in a variety of ways, both in human form and in the form of the Universe.

Repeat these affirmations to remind yourself of your mother tree and the roots that are supporting you:

I am nourished
on my journey

My roots are growing and
strengthening

I will sprout new growth
when the time is right

I am covered by support

I know I am
going to be okay

Picture your mother tree whenever you start to feel untethered. She will support and guide you.

You are a mirror of nature

CHAPTER 6

How

o you find it easy to go with the flow? Or does decision-making leave you feeling like you are swimming upstream? Trusting that you are being guided and led in the right direction can feel futile at times when patience is in short supply or you are experiencing loss, frustration, or grief. When something isn't working out the way you had hoped or dreamed, it can be tempting to dig your heels in and hold even tighter to that project, relationship, or goal.

Sometimes you do need to be resilient and keep trying, not allowing a few failed attempts to derail you. And then there are times when something doesn't work out because it isn't in alignment with your soul's calling. In both cases, the best thing to do is take a deep breath and surrender to the flow of things. The Universe knows what needs to happen for you to find the next right thing, or for the next right thing to find you. And sometimes that means going through loss, heartbreak, or a change of direction in order to get there.

Get quiet and listen to that still, small voice inside you; trust that what is meant for you will find you.

Observe the flow of your life and think about what you have been through so far that has gotten you to this point. Know that every experience, every gain, and every loss have all had a purpose. Each one has been a drop in the river of your life, forming the stream you are floating on right now.

Try not to push against the current. Instead, allow the flow to carry you along, telling the Universe that you trust where you are being guided. The more you allow the flow to carry you, and the more you trust the process, the more opportunity there is for fantastic things to happen. Don't be surprised when seemingly serendipitous opportunities appear for you. That is the magic of the Universe at work, offering reassurance and encouragement that build up your confidence and say, "Keep going! You are moving in the right direction!"

Reflection

Think about a situation in your life that gives you the sensation of swimming upstream, against the current. How does it make you feel? Circle any of the emotions below that resonate with you:

Afraid	Overwhelmed	Frustrated
Distracted	Sad	Hopeless
Ashamed	Discouraged	Annoyed
Self-conscious	Insecure	Awkward
Anxious	Guilty	Vulnerable
Resentful	Confused	Worried

Now think about a situation, event, or relationship that flows and works easily and effortlessly for you. Circle any of the feelings below that come to mind:

Proud	Energetic	Joyful
Hopeful	Trusting	Connected
Confident	Content	Encouraged
Relaxed	Powerful	Centered
Happy	Calm	Excited
Optimistic	Grateful	Delighted

On the next page, journal a bit about the differences between these two situations, how they contrast in the feelings they bring up, and if comparing the two might help you connect more with your soul and intuition when it comes to making decisions for your life.

How do I feel?

On the following two pages, journal about what you trust. Feel free to come back to these pages over time to add more things you trust. Not every day is the same!

journal between the lines... Too

I am trusting...

Affirmations

Figuring out when to push against the current and when to go with the flow of life is a constant challenge. But when you consistently check in with your soul and take time to listen to your intuition, you will feel a lot less resistance and be happily surprised by the opportunities that come your way.

Repeat these affirmations when you need a reminder to trust the flow of your life:

I know that each
experience has a purpose

I will let the Universe
carry me on my soul's journey

What is meant for me will find me

I trust the flow
of my life

You are being carried effortlessly along on your soul's journey. Trust and know the Universe is leading you to amazing places.

CHAPTER 7

Hope

*I*s there anything more surprisingly magical than a rainbow sighting? Rainbows are experts at catching us off guard and taking our breath away with their stunning beauty. Witnessing one in person feels extraordinary and special, like it was placed in the sky just for you. The first glimpse of those bands of color shooting up from the ground and mingling with the clouds can stop you in your tracks, make your heart skip a beat, and elicit an immediate "Ooh!" of delight.

If you're like me, you usually grab your phone for a quick photo, and you probably share a picture on social media. I can't resist sharing all the rainbow feelings!

The imagery and symbolism of a rainbow resonate with all of us in one way or another. A rainbow is a reminder that beauty and hope still exist and can pop up when you are least expecting them. You never know when a rainbow may appear—it's one of nature's best surprises!

What words and feelings immediately come to mind when you see a rainbow?

Depending on when you discover it, seeing a rainbow can bring up all sorts of reactions. They can spark your childlike imagination (they remind me of my favorite childhood toys), conjure up feelings of whimsy and joy, or summon courage and hope in the face of a challenging situation. A rainbow can feel like a loving wink from a special person you are missing, or a colorful sign from the Universe to let you know you're on the right track and that everything is going to be okay. Rainbows are basically all-occasion hope dealers!

Every day, we are given the opportunity to notice the enchanting and whimsical parts of being human, and rainbows are the Universe's way of saying, "I got you! Here is a little extra magic."

Keep
some room i
heart for
unimag

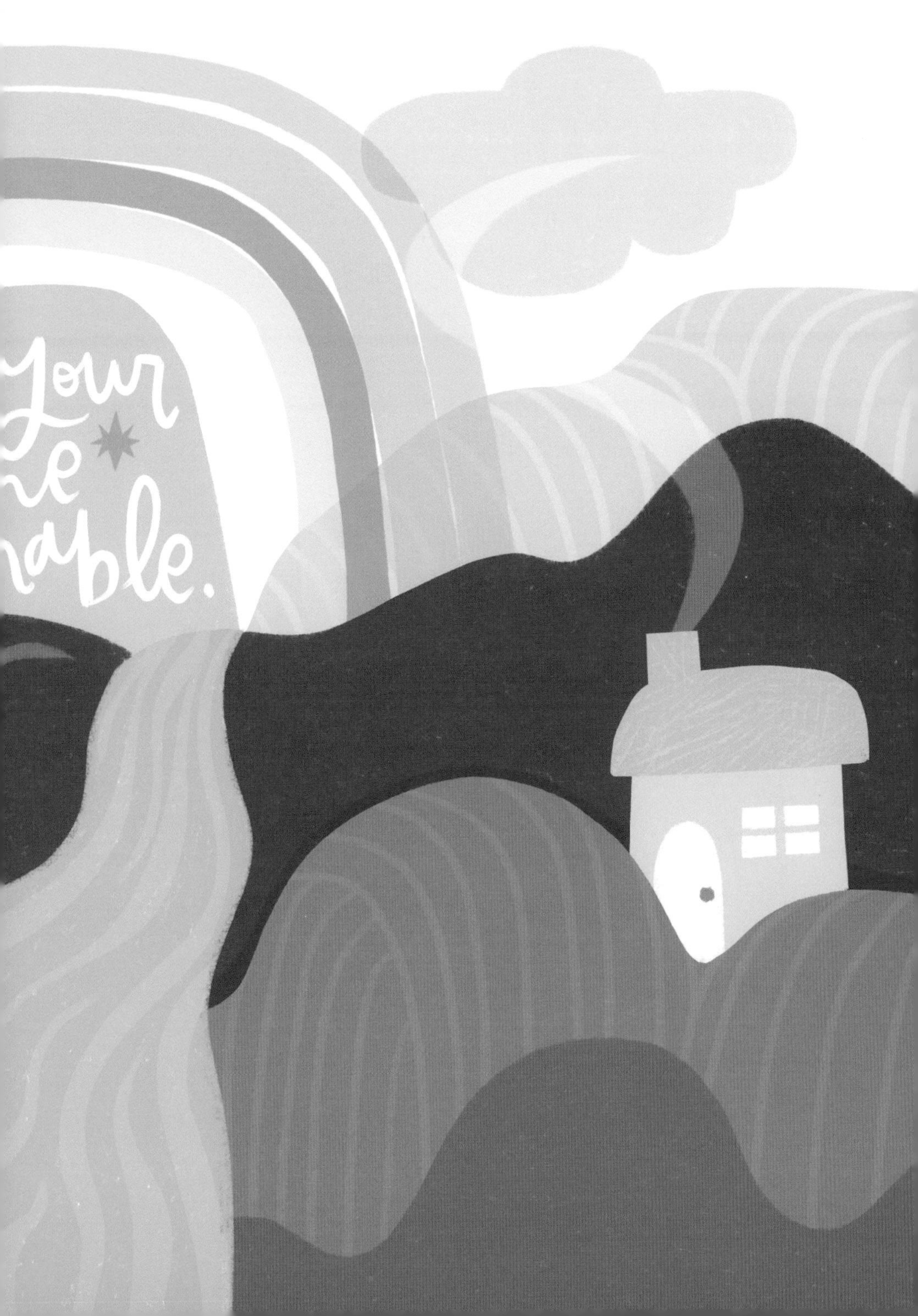
Your
e
able.

Reflection

Think about the last time you saw a rainbow. Was it while you were driving, on a nature walk, or standing at your front door? Do you remember how it made you feel? Was it comforting, magical, awe-inspiring? Think about if you were able to stop and take it in, or if you had only a few fleeting seconds to enjoy it. What words come to mind when you think about the experience?

Journal your reflections on these questions here.

_____

_____

_____

_____

_____

_____

_____

Now think about a time when you needed an extra dose of hope, and something or someone showed up to surprise you in the best of ways, like a sudden rainbow appearing to let you know everything would be okay. Take a few minutes to record that experience here.

_____

_____

_____

_____

_____

_____

_____

_____

_____

_____

Activity: Collage

Let's make a rainbow collage! You can use magazine bits, stickers, patterned paper, markers, and other craft supplies to fill up your rainbow. Coordinate your collage bits with each color of the rainbow.

Affirmations

One of the best parts of nature is the unexpected gifts it offers. Rainbows provide a surprising multicolored dose of hope!

Repeat the following affirmations to remind yourself that there is beauty and encouragement waiting for you around every corner:

I will make space
for magical surprises

I am open to the unimaginable

I will hold on to hope

I trust the Universe to share
beauty when I need it

Know that you will be given the gift of surprising magic from the Universe when you least expect it and most need it. Whether it comes as a literal rainbow or in the shape of help from a friend or a new opportunity, surprises for your soul are always waiting to be discovered.

Surprised
by
Magic

CHAPTER 8

Soar

So many of nature's whimsical gifts require you to stop what you are doing and look up. To take a break from your hectic life and align your gaze with the sky. The landscape above you is constantly changing and offering delight and a connection with nature.

One of the most amazing manifestations of the sky's magnetism is a bird murmuration. Have you ever seen one? It is a mesmerizing sight. I recently witnessed one on an ordinary day driving home from the post office. I was stopped at a red light, and there they were, a flock of birds undulating across the sky, back and forth between the rooftops of the neighborhood houses. Their movements were so graceful and dramatic—even hypnotic! As I drove through a few more lights and two more street blocks, they continued to dance through the sky.

It was one of those ordinary days punctuated by magic. Those are the best, aren't they?

You are in the middle of doing mundane human things, running on autopilot, and then, out of nowhere, nature reminds you to take a break and remember this other realm of existence. It feels weightless and full of possibility.

I was thinking about the phenomenon of a murmuration, and while I'm not sure how they do it—how the birds know when to turn, dive, soar upward, and dive again—it reminded me of how it seems like the Universe works. It orchestrates a million tiny movements to create something magical, unpredictable, and fantastic. You are brought to a place beyond your imagination.

Each daily experience, no matter how small or mundane it might seem, is all movement in this dance that takes you from the starting point to a destination you had no idea was coming.

But then, there you are, right where you are meant to be.

Have you ever experienced something that came together so perfectly and then looked back to see how all the tiny threads of your life conspired together to make it a reality? It feels serendipitous, and yet you know it isn't all by coincidence. The Universe makes it happen. Just like the birds somehow intuitively know when to turn, dive, soar, and dive again, the Universe knows the million little twists and turns that will weave together to push you toward your soul's purpose.

• • •

The Universe orchestrates a million tiny movements to create something magical, unpredictable, and fantastic.

• • •

ts + turns of my life

Reflection

Everyday life can get boring, repetitive, and frustrating at times. It is easy to fall into the trap of wanting the obvious "wow" moments on repeat, to keep things interesting and exciting. But the Universe sends you a quieter version of these moments all the time. All you need to do is calm your mind and pay attention to notice them.

The key is to focus on how each of your daily moments is woven together to lead you in the right direction, to add delight to your day, or to simply bring more good energy into your life.

Think about how the Universe might be conspiring in your favor by sending you signs or connecting you to a person or experience right when it is needed.

_____

_____

_____

_____

_____

_____

_____

Take some time over the next few days to keep track of your daily interactions and experiences and journal about them here. Did the extra red light on your morning commute make it so you ran into a favorite person on your walk through the parking lot? Did you step outside just in time to see a butterfly flit past? Document everything you see and feel during the day, and take note of the unexpected and delightful outcomes that were created.

_____

_____

_____

_____

_____

_____

_____

_____

_____

_____

_____

_____

Activity:
Thank-You Note to the Universe

Think of a time in your life when something worked out in a magical way. Did it feel like the Universe was weaving the perfect threads together for you at just the right time? Or think of something you are hoping will work out for you, and imagine the Universe conspiring on your behalf to make it come to fruition. Write a thank-you note to the Universe that documents how this dream or goal came together. Be as specific with details as you'd like. The Universe loves that!

_____

_____

_____

_____

_____

Affirmations

It is important to take breaks from the monotony of your daily life, and sometimes the Universe makes sure that you do by offering surprises from nature. All you need to do is look up!

Repeat the following affirmations when you need a reminder that all your life's movements are necessary to lead you to your soul's intended destination:

I trust the twists
and turns of my life

The Universe is orchestrating
amazing connections for me

I will remember to look up and
notice nature's magic

Every thread of my life
is being woven into
a fantastic journey

Remember to look up when things feel heavy, see the magic being made in the sky, and know all the twists and turns of your life are being woven together to create something amazing.

CHAPTER 9

Change

*C*hange is an inevitable part of life. Nature reminds us of this in so many ways—seasons transitioning one into another, temperatures fluctuating, plants growing and dying and sprouting again. There is one particular part of nature that is a reminder of constant change while simultaneously offering reassurance of a devoted and reliable presence: the moon.

The moon is always present and yet always changing (at least from our vantage point). When I feel like I'm losing hope about a situation or circumstance, I remind myself of its ways. Behind all the worry, anxiety, and uncertainty, the moon offers an unwavering wholeness.

In doing research for this chapter, I discovered fascinating facts about the moon. It is the only spherical satellite orbiting a terrestrial planet in our solar system, and its presence helps stabilize the earth and moderates our climate. And because of the way the earth and moon are situated and rotating in space, the moon always shows the same face, regardless of the phase it is in.

> The moon is a one-of-a-kind, constant, and calming presence both for our planet and for us as individuals, and it has so many lessons to teach us about navigating life.

One of the moon's most helpful lessons for your soul's journey is that you should allow yourself to sink into and fully accept the idea of phases. You will always, always, *always* be going through different phases in your life. Loud and quiet phases, busy and slow phases, productive and hibernation phases. Some phases may last for days, months, or years, and some may last for only minutes or hours.

There will be times when you feel super energized and ready to jump into a new opportunity—showing your full, glowing presence to the world. And then there will be times when you feel withdrawn and quiet and need to guard yourself from the outside world—just as the new moon keeps itself in the shadows.

You are in a constant cycle of different experiences and emotions.

Each phase serves an integral part in continuing and lengthening the thread of your soul's journey. Allow yourself to feel it all and own it all. Lean into it. Find the deep meaning in the changing nature of life. You are not doing anything wrong. You are a soul experiencing what it is to be human, and it is a crazy ride!

Just as the moon must continually go through an array of phases, your soul must also undergo a variety of cycles and changes in order to feel and be whole.

Reflection

A few chapters back, I shared about the idea of growing the seeds of your dreams and how sometimes it is important to keep things close and quiet until they are ready to be shared. That feeling of being guarded and staying in hibernation mode is what the new moon is all about.

It's okay to need time alone to let your soul rest and regain energy before moving forward with new ideas and goals.

Take some time to journal here about a time you were in a "new moon" phase—or maybe you are in one right now. How can you give yourself grace during this time? How is staying quiet helping your dream take shape?

_____

_____

_____

_____

_____

_____

_____

In contrast, when you are in a "full moon" phase, you feel confident and ready to show yourself to the world. You are prepared to go out and manifest those big dreams! Take some time to journal about a goal, dream, or project you can use full-moon energy to help manifest. You can also use this space as a spot to brainstorm future ideas!

_____

_____

_____

_____

_____

_____

_____

_____

_____

_____

_____

_____

Activity:
Moon Phase Chart

Each phase of the moon offers you words of guidance and different energy for your soul's journey. Look up what the moon phase dates are for the month during which you are reading this chapter. A quick internet search will provide them for you. Document the dates here and then pay attention to how you are feeling, acting, and moving in the world during those times. Pay attention to the phrases listed for each phase and how they may correspond to your life and what you are working toward.

Do you notice any similarities between the moon phase dates and what you are currently experiencing?

How can you use the guidance of each phase to inform the choices you are making and how you are taking care of yourself?

How can you plan ahead to use the energy of each phase to your advantage?

New: ___/__/__   Waxing crescent: ___/__/__

First quarter: ___/__/__   Waxing gibbous: ___/__/__

Full: ___/__/__   Waning gibbous: ___/__/__

Third quarter: ___/__/__   Waning crescent: ___/__/__

New

new beginnings
+ fresh starts

Waxing crescent

create new
intentions

first quarter

take action toward
goals + dreams

waxing gibbous

choose the best
for your present

all the Phases

full

release intentions
to the Universe

waning gibbous

celebrate
abundance

third quarter

give yourself
grace

waning crescent

surrender to
the Universe

Affirmations

Embracing change can be one of the most challenging parts of being human. But when you are able to accept the dynamic nature of life, you can be present with each moment and know, no matter what is happening around you, that there is always an unwavering wholeness available to support you.

Repeat the following affirmations when you need a reminder that the cycles and changes of life are normal and that you are going to be okay:

In every phase I am whole

I will honor the cycles of my
soul's journey

I have a constant source of hope
available to me

The moon is my faithful
reminder of a devoted and
reliable presence

Every time you see the moon, thank it for its guidance and stabilizing energy. It is ever present and always there for you.

CHAPTER 10

Rest

*T*here are times when your body, mind, and soul simply need to rest. You may be weary and feel unable to take your next steps, or perhaps your to-do list is so overwhelming that you can't decide what to do first.

It might sound counterproductive, but rest can be the best remedy for an overwhelmed mind and a too-long list of things to get done. It can be as simple as five minutes or as extravagant as a whole day (or even longer!). Truly, taking rest is crucial to the health of your soul and to achieving your dreams.

I have had so many instances when I've allowed myself to lie down for a nap, read a book, enjoy an extra-long shower, or take a drive, and out of nowhere an idea or insight will introduce itself.

It's like a collaboration between my soul and the Universe—the best kind of partnership.

Resting on my cloud

When I think about how rest and nature intersect, clouds are one of the first things that pop into my mind. Cloud gazing is one of my go-to relaxation activities. Sometimes it looks like sitting on my front porch with coffee mug in hand, staring up at the white cotton-candy wisps floating across the sky. Or I may be relaxing in my car at my favorite spot—the pond in our local park—watching the ducks and then finding myself completely distracted by the clouds above me, so still and calm, a show of bright white punctuating the blue sky.

If you are constantly moving, doing, and thinking, your soul doesn't have time to catch up and connect with the energy that is always out there waiting for an opportunity to work with you.

Doing something that is relaxing and that brings you peace allows you to connect in a deeper way with your internal compass and feel your way through what your soul needs in that exact moment.

Let the clouds teach you their ways.

They know how to float, be still, and move with the winds they are given. They will give your imagination and soul a place to rest.

louds teach you

ways

Reflection

When we are constantly on the go, it can be super hard, if not impossible, to tune in to what our soul wants and needs. The concept of burnout is discussed a lot these days, and it is so very real. Sometimes our body and mind will force us to rest when we go too hard for too long.

Think about a time in your life when it felt like everything was moving too quickly and you were overwhelmed. What was hectic about this time, and what was unhelpful?

Did you have uncomfortable physical sensations? Was it hard to focus or concentrate, or were you forgetting things or making mistakes? These are all sure signs that you needed to pause, evaluate your situation, and find a way to give your mind and body some rest.

On the flip side, were you able to do anything during that time that was helpful and rejuvenating to recover from the experience? Looking back, are there things you could have done that you didn't have in your rest toolbox at the time?

_____

_____

_____

_____

_____

Think about activities or practices that bring you joy. They can be as simple as a enjoying a mug of your favorite coffee or tea, listening to your favorite music, or going on a nature walk. Take some time here to brainstorm rejuvenating and helpful practices you either used during a burnout time or could use in the future. Write down anything that comes to mind!

_____

_____

_____

_____

_____

_____

_____

_____

_____

_____

Remember that while life will always include hectic and stressful times, the helpful and rejuvenating practices you develop are crucial to keeping yourself balanced and in alignment with your soul. You might want to keep this list you've created on hand as a reference and reminder of the calming tools you have available to you.

Activity:
Comfy Cloud Meditation

Find a spot outside or near a window where you can comfortably watch the clouds. Make sure you are wearing cozy clothing; if you would like, you can up the comfy factor by surrounding yourself with pillows or wrapping yourself in a soft blanket. If you can't watch the real thing, search for a video of clouds online, or simply close your eyes and envision a sky full of puffy, bright clouds.

Take a few deep breaths to relax and calm your mind. Focus on watching the clouds travel across the sky, floating and letting nature move them along.

Choose a single cloud and envision it enveloping you like a big, cozy pillow, reassuring and comforting you, giving you time to rest and float along in its soft embrace.

How does the cloud feel? What color is it? Imagine your body completely supported and cushioned by your cloud. Thank it for allowing you the time to rest your soul and calm your mind. Take as much time as you need to allow every part of your body to drop into its soft nooks and folds. There is no part of you that is not supported.

Stay here as long as you need.

Watch from your comfy seat as other clouds float past you across the sky. Return to your cloud whenever the world feels heavy and overwhelming. Know you have this spot to completely relax whenever you need it.

cloud gazing in progress

Affirmations

Rest is crucial to a soul-centered life. If you need permission, I am giving it to you now. Take the time you need to disconnect from the hectic world around you and find a place of cozy stillness and comfortable quiet.

Repeat these affirmations when you need a reminder that it is not only okay, but also necessary, to rest:

I give myself
permission to rest

My best ideas can be found in a
place of relaxation

I can find a place
of calm for my soul

I am supported
in my soul's journey

Nature gives me an outlet
for soul care

Your soul will thank you when you take time to truly rest and connect with nature and the positive energy it is sending your way. Know that you have permission to pause and simply be present with yourself.

I give myself permission to rest

CHAPTER 11

Shine

Your unique presence, just like the sun, provides a light and nourishment that is much needed in the world. There may be times when you struggle with letting your light shine. It can be challenging and even scary to allow your full self out into the world and to show up authentically. You may worry what other people will think or if they will accept you. But if you are doing the work your soul is meant to be doing, there is absolutely no reason to hide in the shadows. You are here for a reason! Surround yourself with people who celebrate your light and help you shine. There is only one you, and you are worth celebrating!

There may be days when you doubt this. Maybe today is one of those days. You will have times where your light is clouded and you aren't sure what your purpose is. And then there will be days when your confident light beams brightly—when you know you are being supported and guided by the Universe.

I'm here to tell you that on each and every one of those days—the cloudy and the bright—your light can be a constant source of positive energy for the world.

I wrote this chapter in April, when the weather is quite unpredictable in Indiana. My husband and boys were growing several different vegetables for the first time; because the weather had been so cold and overcast, we moved the seeds in their starter containers to a makeshift plant stand in our family room, next to a window, so they could stay warm while also getting whatever sunlight decided to peek out. The broccoli seeds were the first to sprout, tiny spring-green buds peeking out above the soil. They knew the sun was there even though it wasn't fully revealing itself. They took in what was available to them, and they thrived. It is such a wonder to watch that process happen!

Just like those tiny broccoli buds, we literally need the sun and its energy to grow and survive. We know it is there, every day, keeping us going. The sun's presence is felt even when it is covered by clouds. The sun is always there, feeding the earth and everything living upon it—feeding you, and encouraging you to shine right back at it.

• • •

Your unique presence, just like the sun, provides a light and nourishment that is much needed in the world.

• • •

Surround
with
who celebrate

how I
can shine
my light...

1.

2.

3.

4.

5.

Reflection

Have you ever taken the time to think about how you contribute light to the world? How do you share positive energy with others? Take some time to think about the ways you show up in the world with an encouraging light. Are there ways you haven't been doing this that you would like to start doing?

In the rays of the sun on the facing page, document both the things you are currently doing and the things you aspire to do that add light and positive energy to the world.

Over the coming weeks and months, jot down moments when you feel you are shining brightest. Look back at this list on cloudy days to remind yourself that you can shine.

_____

_____

_____

_____

_____

_____

Activity: Sunlight Meditation

There are two specific times of the day that offer a ton of magic and connection with nature: when the sun is rising and when it is setting. Choose either of these times to set aside a few minutes to practice this meditation.

Find a comfortable seat either outside, in front of a window, or wherever you can view the sunrise or sunset. Do your best to find a spot where you can be facing the sun. Start by fixing your gaze toward the sun itself (being careful never to look directly at it!). As you do this, take a few deep breaths, relax into your seat, and say a thank-you to the sun for all it does for you:

> Thank you, sun, for your
> light and nourishment.

Now slowly start to move your gaze upward. Focus on the layers of light coming up from the horizon, emanating from the sun. Notice how the intensity of the light and colors changes as you move your eyes away from the sun and up into the broad sky. What colors do you see? What textures? Are the layers of color mingling with the clouds or doing other magical things? Take a few more deep breaths and say:

> Thank you, sun, for
> showing me your magic.

Now find a spot in the sky that is speaking to you the most. Perhaps it is a color that is drawing you in, or a particular composition that feels comforting. Fix your eyes on that spot as you breathe deeply and intentionally. Now, say:

Thank you, sun, for providing a daily source of delight and comfort for me.

Take as much time as you need, letting the view of the sunrise or sunset feed your soul and relax your mind. Remember that this experience is available to you almost every day, whenever you need to come back to your gratitude for the sun and its nourishment.

Affirmations

It can be tempting to hide your light from the world, and it can feel vulnerable to share your full, authentic self. Take a cue from the sun to encourage yourself to wash the world in your own personal light.

Repeat the following affirmations when you're feeling unsure about letting your light shine brightly:

I bring a unique light to the world

I will surround myself with people who celebrate my light

I can show up authentically

I will take what is available to me with gratitude and I will thrive

The world needs your bright, authentic light. This is your permission to illuminate wherever you are with your own unique glow.

Show your
brightest

Self
to the
world

CHAPTER 12

Believe

Do you believe there are unseen forces conspiring in your favor every moment of every day, guiding your soul in the right direction? Perhaps you have had an experience when you felt or knew that you were in the right place and that things were coming together in a way that was out of your control but that you trusted completely. It is a strange and comforting sensation!

I've had a few moments in my life when I have experienced this unseen but completely known guidance. The best way I can describe it is a reassuring feeling of knowing. Regardless of your current circumstances and fear of the unknown, you simply know everything is going to work out. It's like having a shared secret held between the Universe and your soul. It may sound a bit ridiculous if you haven't experienced it before, but the mystery and magic become very real once you've found yourself smack dab in the middle of a soul-plus-Universe connection. There is absolutely nothing like it. It feels miraculous and yet simultaneously not surprising all at.

Air, in a way, has similar qualities to the Universe itself.

Air is all around you. It fills every available open space with its energy and presence. It isn't normally visible, but you are aware of its existence every time you breathe it into your lungs, feel it blow against your face, or watch it rustle the leaves on a tree. Air is a source of life, support, and, often, change. Sounds a lot like the Universe, right?

Air and the Universe are two of the most powerful unseen forces. Every once in a while, they will give you proof of their existence. But, more often, they are hanging out in the background, always doing their thing—filling your lungs, guiding your path. They know what their jobs are, and they both do them well.

There is something so magical about an invisible force that makes its presence known and that offers an unfailing sense of trust in how and where you are being guided. There is magic and delight in that mystery!

Do you feel the Universe leading you in the right direction?

The more you take time to quiet your mind and tune in to the positive energy surrounding you, the more you will be certain of its presence.

Tune in to energy Surrounds

the positive

that

you

Reflection

Has there been a time in your life when you felt the presence of unseen forces guiding you? This can often happen when you are in a tough, scary, or unsure season of life. Did you feel or sense things around you? Did people or other types of support show up exactly when you needed them? Write about a time like this below.

_____

_____

_____

_____

_____

Are you currently in a season where you could use extra guidance for the path ahead? Journal about that here and ask the Universe for the additional support you need to keep you on the right track.

_____

_____

_____

_____

_____

Pay attention to signs of support you notice from the Universe, and document them here. This can be anything that stands out to you as feeling encouraging and unique. It could be a repeated number, something in nature, a song, a feeling, or a person showing up for you. Documenting these things can help you be more aware and open to noticing them in the future!

_____

_____

_____

_____

_____

_____

_____

_____

_____

_____

_____

_____

_____

Activity:
Positive Energy Meditation

This meditation is the perfect one to choose when you are overwhelmed by the outside world or feeling unsupported in your soul's journey. It is a reminder that you are constantly surrounded by positive energy.

Find a quiet and comfortable spot to sit and relax. Take a few moments to calm your mind, and take a few deep breaths. Focus on how your body feels; make any adjustments where you feel tense or uncomfortable.

Close your eyes and focus your attention to the space around you.

Think about the atmosphere and the air. How does it feel? What is the temperature? Does the air feel light or dense? Do any colors or imagery come to mind? Focus on how the atmosphere is enveloping you with life-giving air.

Now take a deep breath in and picture the air filling your lungs. How does the air feel as it enters your body? Picture the color and energy of the air. Perhaps it is yellow or pink, and it might have a bright light or a sparkle. Let the air sit in your lungs for a moment before you exhale, and picture it filling your body with light and life.

Now imagine the positive energy of the Universe partnering with the air to fill your lungs and entire body with an all-encompassing sensation of life-giving comfort and glowing encouragement. When you exhale, envision the same positive energy and beautiful light and color filling the space around you.

positive energy

As you inhale, say this phrase to yourself in your mind:

The air and the Universe are enveloping me
with their care and support. I am surrounded
by magic and life-giving energy.

As you exhale, say this phrase to yourself in your mind:

Thank you, air, for filling my lungs and
giving me life. Thank you, Universe, for
supporting and guiding my journey.

Repeat this process as many times as you need to feel relaxed,
encouraged, and guided. Sit with the feeling of being enveloped by
colorful and positive energy.

Affirmations

When life feels out of control and you are unsure what is coming next, it is easy to want visual confirmation that you are on the right track.

Repeat these affirmations when you need a reminder that unseen support is always available to you:

I can allow myself to trust
in unseen guidance

I will tune in to the positive
energy surrounding me

I believe all is coming together
for the best outcome

The Universe is giving
life to my dreams

Just like knowing air is constantly surrounding you and giving you life, remember that the Universe is present as well, guiding your path and giving breath to your dreams.

Meet the Author

Hi there! I'm Mandy Ford, an illustrator, lettering artist, graphic designer, teacher, and creative soul living in Indiana with my husband and twin boys. After a 15-year absence from drawing, a magical series of events led me back to the practice of creating art that brings my soul alive. I specialize in whimsical artwork that encourages you to live an authentic, joyful life. I love connecting with people and using my art and my voice to help others feel seen, cared for, and loved. You can find my artwork in coloring books, printables, art prints, stickers, and other gift items, as well as in murals in my hometown. I'm also the founder of the Soul Care Creatives Club. My past partnerships have included Paper House Productions, Legacy Publishing, *Spirituality & Health* magazine, Mohawk Rugs, and Inked Brands. Learn more at *www.mandyford.co* and connect with me on social media @mandyfordart.

Index

Tear + Share
Affirmation Cards

Ignite **your** spark

Show your brightest

Self to the world

It is all a miracle and it all matters

In the coming pages, you will find 16 cards to tear and share.

Whether you are looking for a little reminder for yourself or want to share them with others, you can use these cards to brighten your day and remind yourself of what's important.

• • •

Some ideas on how you can use them:

- Keep them in your wallet for daily inspiration.
- Punch a hole in a corner and use them as gift tags.
- Leave them behind for a stranger to find.

Tear + Share Affirmation Cards

how I can shine my light...

Filling your Lungs Guiding your path

Always present. Always changing.

Ignite your spark

I will embrace change and accept the dynamic nature of life. I will honor the cycles of my soul's journey.

The Universe is breathing life into my dreams. I will allow myself to trust in unseen guidance. I will tune in to the positive energy surrounding me.

I will grow the flame of my dream one spark at a time. I am surrounded by encouragement. The Universe is sending me exactly what I need.

I trust the twists and turns of my life. Every thread of my life is being woven into a fantastic journey.

Show your brightest Self to the world

I will Surrender to the flow

N

W E

S

I trust the Universe to guide me.

Protect your growing dream

I know that each experience has a purpose, and what is meant for me will find me. I will let the Universe carry me on my soul's journey.

I bring a unique light to the world. I will surround myself with people who celebrate my light, and I will show up authentically.

I will keep my dream close and quiet. I will protect my dream and surround it with positive energy while it grows.

I trust that the Universe has wonderful gifts to give me. I know I am worthy of a life full of meaning and enjoyment.

It is all a miracle and it all matters

Surprised by Magic

What is the dream of your soul?

I will remember to look up and notice nature's magic.
I know that each daily experience, no matter how small or mundane, is taking me toward my dreams.

I am on a grand adventure. Every step of my journey is important.
I will practice being present in each moment.

I was created for a purpose, and I can manifest a life of meaning.
I am worthy of my dreams.

I will hold on to hope. I trust the Universe to share beauty when I need it, and I will make space for the unimaginable.

how I
can shine
my light...

Like the moon, in every phase I am whole. I will adapt to my changing needs and feelings.

The world needs my bright, authentic self. I will find ways to illuminate wherever I am with my own unique glow.

My dream is sacred, and it is worthy of my care and support as well as the care and support of others.

I give myself permission to rest and recharge. When I need to, I will disconnect from the hectic world and find a place of cozy, comfortable quiet.

BETTER DAY BOOKS®

HAPPY · CREATIVE · CURATED

Business is personal at Better Day Books. We were founded on the belief that all people are creative and that making things by hand is inherently good for us. It's important to us that you know how much we appreciate your support. The book you are holding in your hands was crafted with the artistic passion of the author and brought to life by a team of wildly enthusiastic creatives who believed it could inspire you. If it did, please drop us a line and let us know about it. Connect with us on Instagram, post a photo of your art, and let us know what other creative pursuits you are interested in learning about. It all matters to us. You're kind of a big deal.

it's a good day to have a better day!®

www.betterdaybooks.com
better_day_books